SCOUTING JOKE BOOK

First published 2011 by Macmillan Children's Books
a division of Macmillan Publishers Limited
20 New Wharf Road, London N1 9RR
Basingstoke and Oxford
Associated companies throughout the world
www.panmacmillan.com

ISBN 978-0-330-54490-0

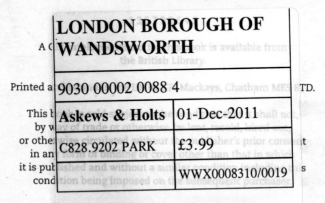

www.scouts.org.uk/join

THE SCOUTING JOKE BOOK

Illustrated by
David Parkins

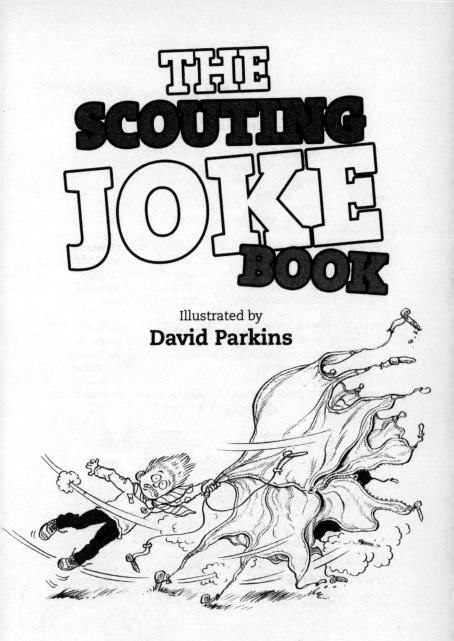

MACMILLAN CHILDREN'S BOOKS

Phil: Our camp meals are full of UFOs.

Charlotte: What do you mean?

Phil: Unidentified Frying Objects.

Why are Scouts so dizzy?

Because they're always doing good turns.

Did you hear about the Scout who tried to swim across the lake?

He got halfway to the other side, then decided he was too tired, so he turned around and swam back again!

What is brown and sticky?

A stick.

First Scout: I bet I can jump higher than that tent.

Second Scout: Have you ever seen a tent jump?

What do you call a boomerang that won't come back?

A stick.

What's brown and nutty?

Squirrel poo.

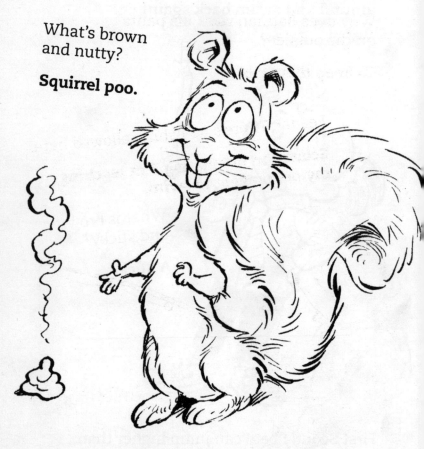

Why do toadstools grow close together?

They don't need mushroom.

Who invented fire?

Some bright spark.

Why does Batman wear his pants
on the outside?

To keep them clean.

Leader: There's no fishing allowed here.

**Scout: I'm not fishing, I'm teaching
my pet maggot to swim.**

Leader: Who can tell me how to start a fire with two sticks?

Scout: Make sure one of them's a match.

Scout: How long will my sausages be?

Leader: About ten centimetres.

What tea do footballers drink?
Penal-tea.

Why do footballers carry handkerchiefs?

Because they're always dribbling.

Why do people
play football?

For kicks.

What do you call a space magician?

A flying sorcerer.

When's an astronaut's main meal?

Launch time.

How do you get a baby astronaut to sleep?

You rock-et.

What do you get if you cross a chicken with a dog?

Pooched eggs.

How do hens encourage their sports teams?

They egg them on.

Who sleeps with their shoes on?

Horses.

What game do cows
play at parties?

Moosical chairs.

How do fish communicate with each other?

By sea-mail.

What do birds eat for breakfast?

Tweet-a-bix and shredded tweet.

What do you get if you cross a
hedgehog with stinging nettles?

Extremely sore hands.

Leader: Have a look in
that tent over there,
you'll see a ten-foot
snake.

**Scout: Don't be silly,
I know snakes don't
have feet.**

What bird is always
out of breath?

A puffin.

What do you get if you cross a football team
with an ice cream?

Aston Vanilla.

Why can't a car play
football?

It only has one boot.

Why did the football quit the team?
It was tired of being kicked around.

Ben: Did you hear the joke about the rope?

Rob: No, why?

Ben: Oh, skip it.

What do you get from nervous cows?

Milk shakes.

Why do birds fly south in winter?

Because it's too far to walk.

Two goldfish
were in their tank. One turned
to the other and said,

**'You man the gun,
I'll drive'.**

16

Jack: You've got holes in your shorts.

Ben: No I haven't!

Jack: Then how did you get your legs in them?

Knock, knock!

Who's there?

Lass.

Lass who?

That's what cowboys use, isn't it?

Why did the cat join the Red Cross?

It wanted to be a first-aid kit.

What do you call a man with a large
black and blue mark on his head?

Bruce.

What do you call a woman with a weight on
one side of her head?

Eileen.

What is the wettest animal in the world?

A reindeer.

If a crocodile makes shoes, what does a banana make?

Slippers.

What's a crocodile's favourite game?

Snap.

Why did the cat sit on the computer?

To keep an eye on the mouse.

Why did the dinosaur cross the road?

Because the chicken hadn't been invented yet.

Why don't grasshoppers go to football matches?

They prefer cricket matches.

What did the mummy say to the detective?

'Let's wrap up this case.'

Why are mummies so good at keeping secrets?

Because they keep everything under wraps.

What's a vampire's favourite soup?

Scream of tomato.

Why did Robin Hood only rob the rich?

Because the poor didn't have anything worth stealing.

Why did Henry VIII have so many wives?

He liked to chop and change.

Why did knights in armour practise a lot?

To stop them from getting rusty.

Mum caught William with the cake tin.

'And what do you think you're up to?' she asked.

'I'm up to my sixth scone,' he replied.

Helen: I hear your brother is very interested in energy conservation.

Laura: Yes, he conserves all the energy he possibly can!

Doctor, Doctor, sometimes I feel like a marquee and sometimes I feel like a teepee.

I think you're too tense.

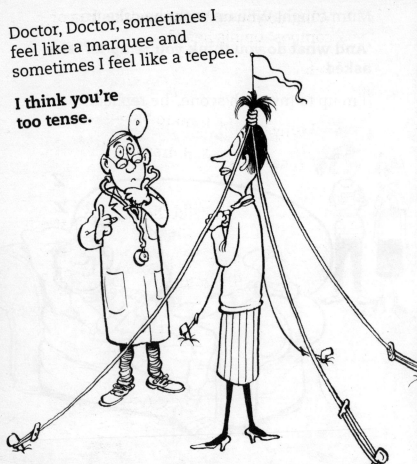

Doctor, Doctor, can you help me out?

Certainly, which way did you come in?

Doctor, Doctor, I feel like a needle.

Yes, I can see your point.

What do you call a man with a bag of compost on his head?

Pete.

Why did the tomato blush?

It saw the salad dressing.

Why did the toilet paper roll down the hill?

Because it wanted to get to the bottom.

What kind of food do maths teachers eat?

Square meals.

Laura: Why are you sitting in the rabbit hutch?

Anna: Because I want to be the teacher's pet.

Why did the teacher wear sunglasses?

Because her pupils were so bright.

Why is it difficult to hold a conversation with a goat?

It always butts in.

What do you call a woman with a storm on her head?

Gail.

What do you call a man with a car number plate on his head?

Reg.

Jenny: Mum, this egg tastes funny.

Mother: Then why aren't you laughing?

Why shouldn't you tell an egg a good joke?

It might crack up.

What happened when the red sauce chased the brown sauce?

It couldn't ketchup.

Leader: If you had five chocolate bars, and your friend asked you for one, how many would you have?

Scout: Five.

A Cub threw a large ball of plasticine at me ... I didn't know what to make of it.

Did you hear the joke about the fart?

You don't want to, it stinks!

How do you greet
a three-headed
monster?

**'Hello, hello,
hello.'**

What is a monster's
favourite bean?

A human bean.

What do you call a lost
monster?

A where-wolf.

What do sad fir
trees do?

Pine.

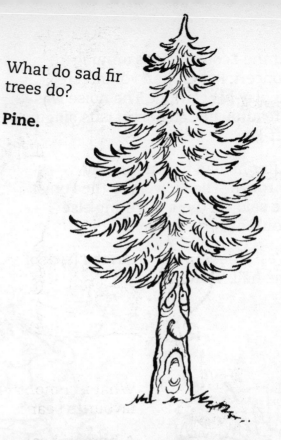

Scout 1: What's the difference between a
sandwich, a bus and a tube of glue?

Scout 2: I don't know.

Scout 1: Well, you can eat a sandwich but you
can't eat a bus.

**Scout 2: Yes, but what about the tube of
glue?**

Scout 1: Ah, I thought that was where you'd
get stuck.

At the Scout Group's annual concert, Robert had volunteered to play his clarinet. The noise was dreadful, like a choir of cats singing off-key.

After he had blown his way through 'The Flowers of the Forest' he said, 'Is there anything else you'd like me to play?'

'Yes!' cried a voice from the back of the hall. 'Dominoes!'

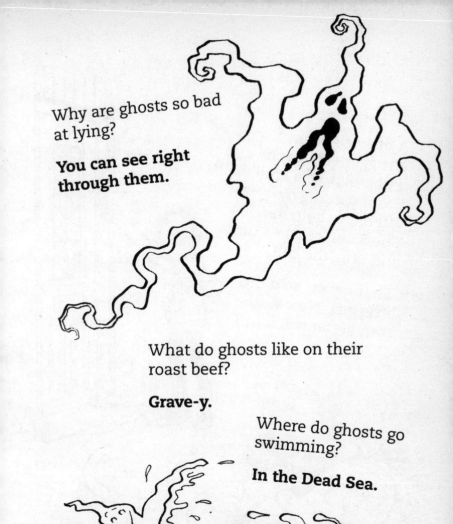

Why are ghosts so bad at lying?

You can see right through them.

What do ghosts like on their roast beef?

Grave-y.

Where do ghosts go swimming?

In the Dead Sea.

A little girl was
struggling to reach
a doorbell, so a kind
Scout passing by
offered to help her.
The Scout reached up
and rang the bell.

'Thank you,' said the
little girl. 'Now we'd
both better run for it!'

Why was the skeleton always left out in judo?

Because he had no body to go with.

Why wouldn't the skeleton take up parachuting?

He didn't have the guts.

Why did the snowman say 'Now you see me, now you don't' when crossing the road?

He was on a zebra crossing.

What's a vampire's favourite dessert?

Leeches and scream.

What's a vampire's favourite fruit?

A blood orange.

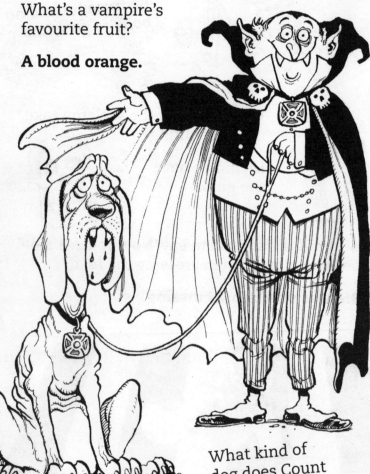

What kind of dog does Count Dracula have?

A bloodhound.

Why is a river rich?

**Because it has
two banks.**

Leader: Eat your greens, they're good for your skin.

Scout: But I don't want green skin!

Sam: What's green, dangerous and grows in fields?

Tim: I don't know.

Sam: Grass.

Tim: But why is it dangerous?

Sam: Because it's full of blades.

What is the best part of a boxer's joke?

The punch line.

What did the peanut report to the police?

That he'd been assaulted.

Why didn't the dog want to play tennis?

It was a boxer.

Why was the alien such a good gardener?

Because he had green fingers.

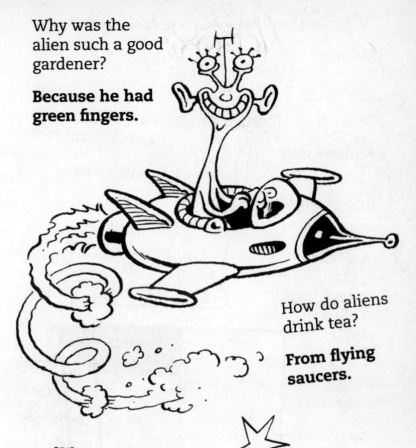

How do aliens drink tea?

From flying saucers.

Why did the Martian go to the optician?

He had stars in his eyes.

What do cornflakes wear on their feet?

Kellogs.

What kind of biscuit can fly?

A plane one.

What's green, hairy and
goes up and down?

**A gooseberry in
a lift.**

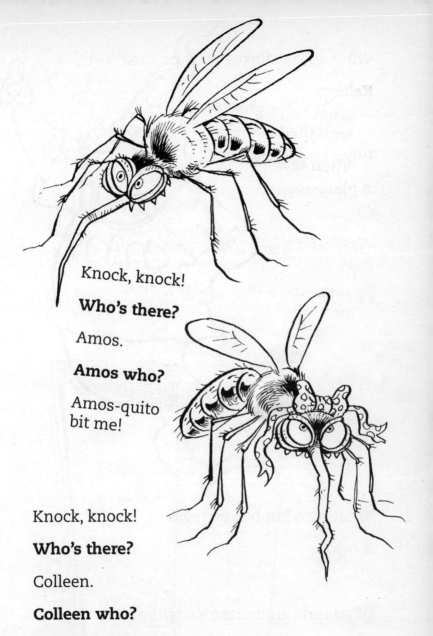

Knock, knock!

Who's there?

Amos.

Amos who?

Amos-quito
bit me!

Knock, knock!

Who's there?

Colleen.

Colleen who?

Colleen yourself up, it's time to eat.

What helps ghosts
with their games?

Their team spirit.

What runs but has no legs?

A tap.

What runs around a field without moving?

A fence.

Scout 1: I've just touched some nettles.
Scout 2: That was rash.

Knock, knock!

Who's there?

Dan.

Dan who?

Dan druff.

What's small, round,
white and giggles a lot?

A tickled onion.

What do you call a
woman with a tortoise
on her head?

Shelley.

What do you call a Scout
camping on a beach?

Sandy.

What do you call a Scout
hiding in a pile of leaves?

Russell.

Mother: Yesterday there were twelve jam tarts in the cupboard, but today there is only one. Why?

Alice: I don't know, I suppose it must have been right at the back where I couldn't see it.

Father: Eat your carrots, Lewis, they're good for your eyes.

Lewis: How do you know?

Father: Well, have you ever seen a rabbit wearing glasses?

Grandma: You've left all your crusts, Edward. When I was your age, I ate every one of mine.

Edward: Do you still like crusts, Grandma?

Grandma: Yes.

Edward: OK then, you can have mine.

What do you get if you eat baked beans and onions at camp?

Tear gas.

Mum: My goodness! Scrape that mud off your shoes before you come in, Chris.

Chris: But Mum, I'm not wearing any shoes . . .

Why did the Scout cross the road?

Because he was following the chicken.

Leader: What should you do if you get locked out of your house?

Scout: Sing until you get the right key.

Neighbour: I've lost my dog, what shall I do?

Scout: Why don't you put an advert in the local paper?

Neighbour: Don't be silly, dogs can't read.

What do you call two robbers?

A pair of nickers.

Doctor, Doctor, I feel like a pack of cards!

I'll deal with you later.

Doctor, Doctor, I feel like a guitar.

Sit down while I make some notes.

Doctor, Doctor, I think I'm invisible.

I can't see you right now.

Oscar: Did you go to Mike's party?

Kate: No, the invitation said 'four to eight' and I'm nine.

Why do church bells never send emails?

They'd rather give each other a ring.

Why didn't the musical instruments email each other?

They preferred to write notes.

Why are adults boring?

Because they're groan-ups.

Why did the Joneses call both their sons Edward?

Because two Eds are better than one.

What do you call a boy wearing headphones?

Anything you like, he can't hear you!

Why did the one-eyed alien teacher give up his job?

He didn't see the point in carrying on with just one pupil.

Why did the King go to the Dentist?

To get his teeth crowned.

Why couldn't the young witch write a proper letter?

She hadn't learned to spell.

Deer Mum

Why was the robot
so silly?

**He had a screw
loose.**

Why did the computer whizz
need an oil can?

His mouse was squeaking.

Why didn't the computer get
on with the printer?

He wasn't her type.

How can you tell which spiders are the trendiest?

They have their own websites.

What books do owls read?

Hoot-dunnits.

First sheep: Baaa.

Second sheep: Moo.

First sheep: What do you mean, 'Moo'?

Second sheep: I'm learning a foreign language.

What did the rug say to the floor?

Don't move, I've got you covered.

What does a winner of a race lose?

His breath.

What can you hold without touching it?
Your breath.

What's orange
and sounds like a
parrot?

A carrot.

What do athletes eat
for lunch?

Runner beans.

What room has no floors, no walls and no windows?

A mushroom.

What do you call a woman with slates on her head?

Ruth.

What do you call a man with a seagull on his head?

Cliff.

How many skunks does it take to raise a big stink?

A phew.

What nut has no shell?

A doughnut.

What has fifty heads but can't think?

A box of matches.

Which athlete stays
the warmest?

The long jumper.

What's round and white and smelly?

A ping-pong ball.

What ring is square?

A boxing ring.

What sleeps on the sea bed and shivers?

A nervous wreck.

What does the ocean say when it sees the coast?

Nothing, it just waves.

Why did the tide turn?

Because the sea weed.

What do you call an elephant that flies?

A jumbo jet.

Where would you find prehistoric cows?

In a moo-seum.

What's a frog's favourite food?

Lollihops.

What's black
when it's
clean and
white when
it's dirty?

A blackboard.

What do you get
after it's been
taken?

Your photo.

What was King Arthur's
favourite game?

Knights and crosses.

What happened to the boy who swallowed an Oxo cube?

He made a laughing stock of himself.

Why are cavemen similar to teenagers?

They like to go clubbing.

Mike: I heard a new joke yesterday. Did I tell it to you?

James: Is it funny?

Mike: Yes.

James: Then you didn't.